I0621262

French Door to Foyer

Poetry by

Signe Damron

SIGNE:TURE
PUBLISHING

Copyright © 2022 Signe Damron

All rights reserved. This book or any portion thereof may not be reproduced or used in any manner whatsoever without the express written permission of the publisher.

Printing in the United States of America

Cover art and illustrations by Cassidy Rae Marietta
Cover and layout design by Madison Fast

First Printing, 2022

ISBN (Hardback): 979-8-9858825-0-6
ISBN (Paperback): 979-8-9858825-1-3
ISBN (ebook): 979-8-9858825-2-0

Signe-ture Publishing
www.signe-ture.com

In Loving Memory Of:
The late Jack Peterson. A writing mentor who saw greatness in me, pushed me to step outside my comfort zone and thus be a better writer. I am forever grateful.

To my late cousin John Nelson, who was the finest pen-pal, quick witted and a talented writer himself along with my connection to my Norwegian heritage.

Table of Contents

Imaginative Adventure

Acknowledgments:

There is something exceptional and powerful about who our community is, who we lean on and value. I believe it makes a difference in the pursuits we make.

Thank you to the writers group I joined twelve years ago and not only met some amazing people who are still my writing mentors and friends, but who helped me find my writing voice, encouraged me to leap and to share it with the world. To Juli Ocean, who continues to be an amazing writing mentor, teacher and friend. To Robert Blackwell for his wisdom from his own journey of being a self-published poet who is a guiding light and mentor for this new terrain of publishing.

To my wonderful cover artist and illustrator, Cassidy Rae Marietta. She took some ideas I had and turned them into magic! Editing is one of the most important components to making a book complete. To Yashi Bellomy who challenged me while stretching my capacity for critique along this process. To Arthur Morris, for being not only my final proofreader, but also a friend throughout the last 12 years who is always willing to read a new piece, think about it and give me good feedback. I would not have been able to finish this project without you.

A support system is key to any success and mine is bountiful and I am incredibly thankful to every one of you! Becca Oden for her continued support and encouragement. Aaron J Davis for his encouragement and support. Andrea Belanger who helped make this book possible with her creativity in branding and patience with helping me figure out how to execute my goals. Kayla Hughes for willing to read new pieces, give opinions and advice along this process. My layout designer, Madison Fast. My brother, Robert Damron for being one of my biggest cheerleaders.

A special acknowledgment to my mother, Nancy Green. I could not have done this project without your amazing support and believing in me. I am incredibly blessed and thankful to you for everything!

Preface

The pieces in this book started coming together 12 years ago during a time when I was dealing with trauma, taking bold new risks and had just joined a writing group who have since become friends and mentors. While I have been writing longer than 12 years, it is only fitting that this is my first book.

The pieces in French Door to Foyer helped me process through grief, grow and evolve as a writer and a person. It showed me my love for talking to strangers and finding adventure in unexpected places and ways.

observational

Unveiling

Sweeping swells
roll restlessly
with each
foray into deep
conversation.

Anticipation of the next leap
into deeper
Provocative territory;
Shedding layers of the
Perceived guarded.

Revitalization

Roller coaster
deep blue jazz
rhythms
seizing new delicacies
with anticipated
surprises.

Cut to the core
and awaken
an apathetic audience
too far deep
under sea water.

Revitalization
is born unto
every inch of your
weary soul with
momentary
meditation
and a really good dance partner.

Untitled

If anyone is willing to listen
we all have captivating stories.
Freedom is easier than we lead on.

If we all gave more,
cared more,
how different
could this world be?

We point the finger
and never listen to our histories
- we are too smart for that!

How righteous are we really?

Covert Surveillance

People watching has taken a new
turn at a familiar place.
Warm weather
tis the season!
Fresh faces
send
my imagination down the rabbit
hole, only to be lost amongst a
chasm of playful conversation.

Mirage

Stellar
disco balls
unlit,
hover above unexpected
crowds.
Illusions twist and deceive
some into thinking
that magic is only
reserved for dictated entities.

Intrigued

Eyes find their way
in my direction.
Protruding questions
implode as
interest and curiosity
unfolds in my favor.
These eyes never leave
focus but
nothing more occurs.
It is a mystery
that vexes me.

I keep my book
closed awaiting
someone
willing
to step through that line and
open the cover.

Cliques & Cliches

In every crowd
dozens of little worlds operate
with the mindset that everything in their
orbit
is all that matters.
Each spots the other
with the same distaste,
hoping to inch themselves
further away from one another
as if leprosy
were still common.

A Modern Red Sea

appears
in an ocean of drunkenness.
People gather and gawk as if Yoda
just attempted
the moon walk

Peacocks

Are easily detected.
They prance around
in hopes they are recognized by
whom they've been captivated.

Their gait
a strut,
a story with each step.

Untitled

Steady visionaries
with chaotic
tendencies,
frolic
about
in frenzied strides
looking for prey.
Hoping they will be found desirable,
more so than the rest of the lot herding over the only
open watering hole.

Cheer

Beers and belly laughs
bring a comfort
different
from the normality
of the hustle and bustle.

Breathe In

Yellow visions spewing
forth demanding attention.
Chaotic hues of vibrant blues and
greens use their delicate voices to lure
you in.
Humming sound waves
tampering with swirls of color
to lull and captivate you
to admire nature's seductive
trance.
Their end goal is admiration;
a type of worship and appreciation
for life.

Weekend's End

A sweet breeze
caressing and seductive.
The sun's delicate kiss
cascading.
A simple evening
turned splendid,
full of surprise and splendor.

A refreshing beer,
a southern light,
the people watching
makes Sunday night a cheer
like no other.

Monday's imminent arrival
always causes alarm,
but nights like these gives a "fuck you" to tomorrow
with a wide grin.
Tonight we play the role of the gods
and look to the sky with gratitude.
Perfection.

Modern Royalty

'Hims' and 'hers' glide and
weave about one another.
Black has become
the new decor
of prestige,
painted personas of success.

Some walk away with
mystery still intact,
while others ruin the
purpose of the
atmosphere.

Here

Funny vibes
after unexpected downpours
of music jams.
People watching just turned
into every gold diggers
paradise.
Chatter still heard
through backup headphones
as I am jamming to two different languages
toying with my imagination
playful inspirations.

Evening Trippers

Evening trippers congregate,
ready as each beckons
another for more drink.
An atmosphere
for any foodie,
wine and spirits
flow freely in the arena.
With bourbon in hand,
I am enticed with not only a
canvas, but the array of
conversation.
Chatter
needs a bit of dancing to
settle insipid snares.

Seeing Self-Doubt

Resplendence wasted
by distaste for itself.

Beauty that could easily
illuminate a room,
dimmed and drafted out the
doors.
Squandered
in part from ill use,
in part from those who miss
out on the artistically
immaculate, and the
pleasurably soulful.

Sometimes,
we forget to observe and
appreciate;
caught up in ourselves.

Undead

Night comes
waking the dead
has become a sort of art,
while insipid galaxies
stake their claim
to each homebody.
A minority
protests for
release
while
the majority engage
in avid apathy.
The biggest complaint of
those that seek change
seems to
always be
a battle for the majority to see the cause.

Be

It's amazing how easy
it was
to stress
about the nonsense
the world provides
and to forget about
the joy of
the moment
designed to be toyed with.

It took a Saturday afternoon
of grocery shopping,
cooking for hours on end,
wine
and good music
to
enjoy
just being.

Grief

While sitting alone I am
leaden with emotions I am all too unfamiliar
with.
Anxiety
has carved a home
and given me the promise
that it has
no intent to leave.
Strangers are more comforting
than the silence
that once relaxed and rejuvenated
me.

Pondering

Confounded
by the intricacies
of the simplicity
and, yet complexity of this world
and the people in it.

Nostalgia

As my heart yearns for you,
my mind replays
the good.
Logic tells me
set it free.
But, I cannot.
Everything in my being is longing,
craving,
to relive
fresh moments of we.

Guarded

She believes herself awkward
and dull;
using intoxicants
and loud conversation
to veil his glimpses of her
soul. Longing to
untether,
she holds back for fear
of rejection.
He is fascinated by her,
hoping she will gaze
at him and let him in.
A tug of war.
"Are you safe?" Her mind
races, "You intrigue me", he
thinks. He wants to be let in
and
she dreads
what damage could be
done if she does.

Human

Acid rain
batters at my heart
and tells me that I've
been defeated.
I let go in the moment
and become wild.

High & Vine

It was a night with
a Russian man and
Russian vodka.
Nearly a dance,
an unreal
adventure. It was
dangerous
and stupid is what
anyone would have told
me,
I knew that.
I went anyway.
I was violated,
drunk.
I beat the shit out of
him.
Russian boy,
you should have known
I was the wrong
American girl to fuck
with.

Sifting Through

I've been captivated by what I could
be, lost in what I could have.
It's so much easier to take
that route.
Instead of pushing reality to
change, to shift with me.
I've got so much working against
me as I decide
in which haystack to begin looking
for that diamond.

Indigo

Paint my eyes indigo
and let
them burn.
I want to feel
more than
the narcissism
my society
presents as the only reality.

I want to know
if that indigo
holds more;
if that burning
reveals something more.

Yes,
there is more
but we are battered to acknowledge only
our lustful ways.
To do more
could be catastrophic, some might say.

So,
paint my eyes
indigo
and let them burn.

Do it Anyways

Sleepless nights
and anxiety
constrained me.

Chains and whispers
told me
that I am not free;
that pushing for
justice is pointless.

However,
the gift of others
has changed my perspective
and taught me
that courage is
beating the shit out of fear.

On Edge

An eagerness to go
with nothing to do.

Cages

Lost in her thoughts,
day dreams captivating
her attention once
again.

Places out of reach, out
of touch
appeal to her need
to escape.
Reality is so often
seen as a cage
and
freedom
is what she yearns for.

Vibes

Sometimes
all you need is
the medicine
of old school beats
that brings comfort
to it all.

Living in the Moment

Has recently
captured my attention.
A new peace
has nestled
just as the desire to swallow
in restlessness
was starting to take hold.

Just being
is the most pleasurable thing at the
moment.
Turbulent seas engage my mind
on a constant
tipping point,
but the late night dwellings
and peaceful pondering
intrigue
and ensnare my attention.

My ambition will find time to sneak in and disrupt
this vacation.
Until then, I play
with contentment for once.

Let My Mind Wander

In a freedom not bound
by anything tied to
intellectualism. Humor and
mysticism,
come be my friends.
Take me,
mold me,
into your flow.

Blues,
I'm willing to let you navigate
me because I know
chains and bounds
never dictate your style.
Silence has a new
becoming in your presence.
Speaks an intimate volume
that emancipates your loud rebels,
and
sends them to their rightful
holes! Give me this moment,
give me this leisurely
escape.

World in its robust noise
will always be a point,
always a debate.
Give me this rhythm where
creativity abounds in the quiet,
of the soul.

Healing

Poetic streams
flood through
me as I escape
into the vastness
of your splendor.

Rivers of depth
are revealed
in hidden layers,
in the silence of
your presence,
which engulfs
my being.

Exploration

I want to explore
the world,
see it all with new
eyes.
Taste the sun
in places I've never heard of.
Dance to beats of every
creed. Laugh with all
languages; and inherit
wisdom
in unforeseen movements.

Chemistry

Comes out of
nowhere and
side-swipes me; an
unexpected
connection.

It leaves me
allured and
confused.
You aren't my type,
yet you intrigue me.
You listen to me.
You fascinate me.

Intimacy

Your words hypnotize me,
as I spin in an exotic twist.
In the moment,
the dance is magic.
Your lips move
with syllables that speak
to my soul.

I am left breathless,
yearning for more.

June 14th

Sun begins to set;
blue skies
make a Saturday
evening brilliant.
Reheated veggie
pizza and a glass of
milk.
Enjoying the breeze,
humming music
with an indie feel.

Relaxing and
contemplating some of
life's mysteries.

Grace

You
have branded
my back.
Let the waters flow
freely by me,
made the winds
move me
so I would not
fall
and you
held me
even though
I've become
greedy.

Evening Dashes

Hitting the pavement,
through different
speeding veins.
Momentarily weightless,
completely dominating surroundings.
No competition.
YOU are the limelight
and only you
can feel it
from the tips of your fingers and
down through your toes.

Rain pours down your face,
showering you
with kisses so sweet
that stopping would be sinful.
The road is quiet,
the perfect kind of peaceful;
freedom from chaos.

The silence is awakening.

Call to Adventure

The wind beats,
with rhythms that can only be
described in the colors they
bleed.

Pick a color,
ride with it
and see where it whisks you off!
Is it to the blue of the ocean,
the red roofs in the heart of the biggest
cities, or to places still quietly unseen?

If we never set sail,
we will be left only with
our lingering regrets
and nothing to back up those possibilities.

Late Night Thoughts

Sometimes brilliance
is held down
by plastic wrap.
Easy to unwrap
if you aren't deceived
by the illusion
of the not.

Crazy and genius have
comparative moments
depending on what
lines have
been crossed.

Creativity abounds
in the
most unlikely
scenarios.

Being
is an underrated
quality
when the grass is always greener on
the other side

Sunburnt

The sun grinning in sweet
deceit, a perfected temptation,
enticing prey
to bask a little longer,
shed a few more layers,
and allow for sweet kisses
that turn to pungent
and potent forces.

Breezes laugh and mock
The oblivious game
amused by their ignorance.

The sun knows
the necessity it provides
along with the deadly
poison it imparts
when dipped too far.

Untitled

Relinquish all forces of control
and feed the abyss.

Seize

Grip me with your metallic
beats.
Quicken me into ambition more
fiery than burning passion.

Loose Vertebrae

Loose vertebrae
move like magnetic puzzles
pleading for an answer.
Skeletal ridges
tumble and collide,
like typewriter keys.
Loose vertebrae
dance in chaotic ridges.
I see them tantalizing me to come closer and
closer.
Who knew bones were able to hold
sensuality like this?
Hypnotic.

Imagination

Take hold of my
reality and
pierce it with glass.

Joy

She peeks around the corner,
eyes full of life.
Red lips puckered,
innocence flows through her.
"Catch me if you can!"
her body motions,
and you are captivated by
her simple joy.

Dimensions

She dreams in color,
magic moving
round and round.
She dances for
freedom.

Hope
calls to her;
and faith screams
for more.

She is a girl
from another time.
Illusions are her
reality.
The present moment
is not what moves
her.

She sees past
the moment
and looks Impossible
in the eye
and places a bet.

She walks
with confidence
as Impossible
mocks her,
but in the end
Impossible underestimates
the power of faith.

Hopscotch

Whispering melodies
play notes
along the streets of
creativity and logic,
challenging the elite
in their prisms of isolation.
Luring life outside of its boxes.

The innovative
are the ones that dare dance with danger
and tell fear to go fuck itself.

Life shifts
with bull-headed pulls
and feisty
lunges.

Unexpected

The air was hot and thick with
a succulent undertone.
Spices enchanted me
despite the stench
in the overgrown cities
polluted in apathy.
The outskirts here
reminded me of
dreams past and movies
that spoke to
depths I did not know I had,
traveling to such far-off places
just for a glimpse of something real
and different.
These places that
were once magical,
bewitch me further
than I thought they would.
Imagination
always brings something to the table
but reality,
despite criticism,
can often bring more magic than you thought possible.

Two-Step

Innovated two step:
adrenaline on the side of the offense
defense ready in timid form resolute, ready to counter.

The intensity of the crowd
screws with conflicted threats
ready to rip you to shreds
placing bets that often dictate the scarcity or the abundance
of your daily meals.

Innovated two step:
hands
wrapped delicately
for the sole purpose of disciplined chaotic
war.

You know nothing of your opponent.
Holding only the intent to
make sure your powerful blows invoke
the right kind of unconsciousness.

Innovated two step:
whiffs of ecstasy as your body rushes
to survival mode
often mistaken for impending victory.

Innovated two step:
it's Armageddon tonight for as many rounds
as it takes.

Sips of water feel as though heaven
has grazed against your lips.
It's better than the prize you're promised at the end.

Risky

Sweat and cold slap me with paddles.
My lungs burn with each breath.
My eyes feel as though they're being
pierced over and over again.
I think I'm giving Rudolph a run for her
money
with every moment
I stand atop this mountain.
As I peer down the slope with my feet strapped to polished
wood,
I see the forbidden territory
that my ruthless
ambition yearns for.

I inhale deeply, painfully
and…
a moment of silence.
I tip my board
down the slope of the mountain.
Exhilaration!
I am ready!

Open

Break open your lairs
and allow
your mire
to evaporate.
Let the fresh air
come racing in,
filling your sanctuary
with life.

Perfect Unison

Beautiful dresses,
heels from another world
tap to the beat.
Slow at first,
then a partner
arises and to watch them
is like seeing lights
glide
in perfect unison.
They flow steady and smooth,
wild and seductive,
each of them spinning
as an array of colors
fog the room.
Heels and toes tap in
one rhythm
that fascinates
every eye in the room and stirs
curiosity,
which pulls the
timid from
their shelves
and simply asks "Why not?"
and, in that moment
criticism is cast aside
and they are soaked with fun,
knee deep in vulnerability.

New Beginnings

Open yourself up
to something new.
Break free,
no looking back.
Risk it
and let the wind
course through your
hair.
Worry about no
outcome.
The present worries will
expire.
Dwelling leads
nowhere.
Instead,
push through the
doors,
ready to take on the new.

About the Illustrator:

Cassidy Rae Marietta is a visual content curator, illustrator, and painter working out of her mid-century modern home in Columbus, Ohio. With sheets of velvety hues, ornate designs, and expressive figurative elements, her work is focused on creating striking images that showcase the modern woman, dotted with botany and psychedelia. Recurring themes in her work include censorship, social normality, and the raw and undying characteristics of human nature. Her keen eye for color and detail has helped blossom a career that includes collaborations, design, and graphic work for clients around the globe.

www.ingramcontent.com/pod-product-compliance
Lightning Source LLC
Chambersburg PA
CBHW051645120626
46551CB00015B/2218